THE
VICTORIAN KITCHEN
Book of
CAKES & COOKIES

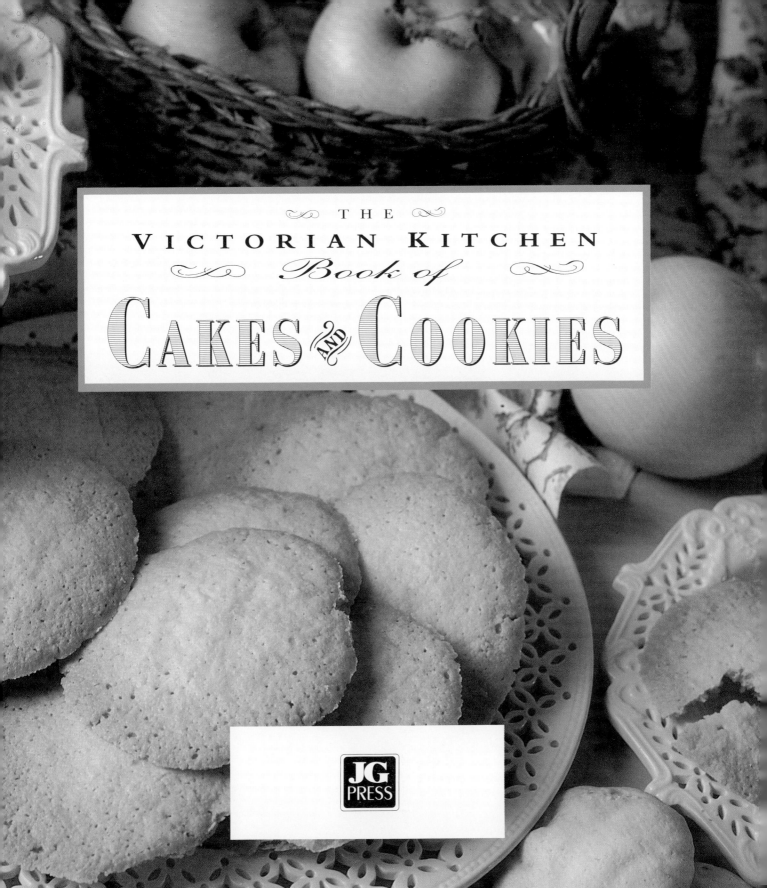

THE
VICTORIAN KITCHEN
Book of
CAKES AND COOKIES

JG PRESS

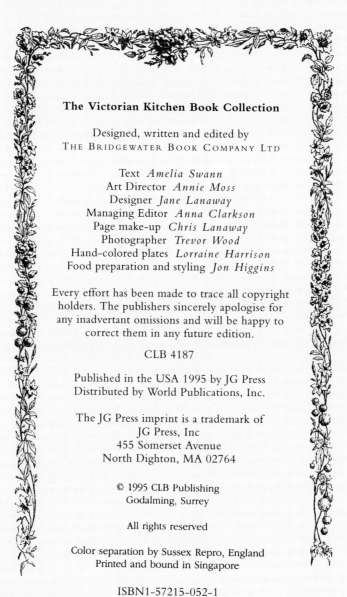

The Victorian Kitchen Book Collection

Designed, written and edited by
THE BRIDGEWATER BOOK COMPANY LTD

Text *Amelia Swann*
Art Director *Annie Moss*
Designer *Jane Lanaway*
Managing Editor *Anna Clarkson*
Page make-up *Chris Lanaway*
Photographer *Trevor Wood*
Hand-colored plates *Lorraine Harrison*
Food preparation and styling *Jon Higgins*

Every effort has been made to trace all copyright
holders. The publishers sincerely apologise for
any inadvertant omissions and will be happy to
correct them in any future edition.

CLB 4187

Published in the USA 1995 by JG Press
Distributed by World Publications, Inc.

The JG Press imprint is a trademark of
JG Press, Inc
455 Somerset Avenue
North Dighton, MA 02764

Color separation by Sussex Repro, England
Printed and bound in Singapore

ISBN1-57215-052-1

CONTENTS

INTRODUCTION

Dost thou think, because thou art virtuous, there shall be no more cakes and ale?

WILLIAM SHAKESPEARE, TWELFTH NIGHT

AFTERNOON TEA AND CAKES was established in England in the 1820s, when the tea plantations in Assam, India, began to yield cheap and plentiful tea. By the time Victoria became queen, it was an indispensable and agreeable daily ritual.

Victorian cooks began to expand their cake repertoire, helped by the introduction of raising agents such as baking powder and bicarbonate of soda in the mid-19th century. For the next century, at least, the tea tables of upper and middle class households were graced by such delicious confections as seed cake, plum cake, savoy cookies, macaroons, meringues, gingerbread, and sponges of all kinds.

A Teatime Selection

The recipes in this book can only show a selection of the many mouthwatering cakes and cookies perfected by the Victorian cook. The recipes are based on authentic sources, adapted for modern tastes and for the smaller families of today.

MRS. BEETON'S CAKE-MAKING HINTS

1 **Break eggs separately into a cup before adding to a mixture, in case any are bad.**
2 **Wash and thoroughly dry all dried fruit.**
3 **Soften butter by warming it gently before creaming it.**
4 **Cover large cakes with a sheet of wax paper during cooking to prevent burning.**
5 **To test a cake's progress in cooking, push a clean knife blade into its center; if it emerges sticky, the cake is not done.**

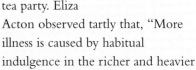

Not everyone approved of this perpetual tea party. Eliza Acton observed tartly that, "More illness is caused by habitual indulgence in the richer and heavier kinds of cakes than could easily be credited by persons who have given no attention to the matter." She was more kindly disposed to meringues, spongecakes and cookies, which she considered to be "the least objectionable." However, this did not prevent her from publishing some of the most delectable recipes for such "sweet poisons" as Fine Almond Cake and Poundcake, adapted versions of which can be found in this book.

RAISING AGENTS

In the mid-19th century, baking powder and bicarbonate of soda were produced commercially. This allowed enterprising cooks to branch out and make light cakes and cookies. Traditionally, the most common raising agents were eggs (for spongecakes) and yeast, which produced rather solid cakes, more like fancy bread than modern cakes.

Cookies & Biscuits

WHAT THE ENGLISH TODAY CALL BISCUITS ARE MUCH BETTER DESCRIBED AS COOKIES. "COOKIE" IS DERIVED FROM THE DUTCH WORD FOR "LITTLE CAKE." IT HAS BEEN USED SINCE THE 18TH CENTURY IN SCOTLAND AND AMERICA, AND IS NOW FINDING ITS WAY BACK TO ENGLAND. THE WORD BISCUIT COMES FROM THE FRENCH *BIS-CUIT* AND ORIGINALLY REFERRED TO VERY DRY PRODUCTS SUCH AS RUSKS OR SEA BISCUITS.

ALL THE CAKES AND COOKIES YOU NEED
FOR A SUMPTUOUS VICTORIAN TEATIME SPREAD

MACAROONS

Macaroons are a light, European confection much appreciated by the Victorians, who loved anything flavored with almond. These are based on Mrs. Beeton's recipe.

INGREDIENTS

3 Egg Whites
2²/₃ cups Ground Almonds
1 cup Sugar
Rice Paper
Flaked Almonds

METHOD

❧ Place the egg whites in a very clean mixing bowl and whisk until they form stiff peaks. Gently fold in the ground almonds and the sugar until they are evenly incorporated.

❧ Spoon the mixture onto baking sheets lined with rice paper using a teaspoon, leaving space between each macaroon to allow them to spread, and place a flaked almond on top of each one.

❧ Bake at 325°F until they turn a light brown color, then remove any excess rice paper and cool on wire racks.

COOK'S TIP

For lighter macaroons, add a little more egg white.

MACAROONS AND LITTLE RATAFIAS

Holy Macaroons

Macaroons were probably invented in Italy, but have been made in France for centuries. After the French Revolution, it became the custom for convent nuns to make and sell them.

Little Maccaroons, sweet as sugar and almonds can make them

✢✢

SIR JAMES GRANT

RATAFIAS

Ratafias are essentially miniature macaroons. The egg white and sugar mixture is piped through an icing bag to make tiny cookies. They get their name from ratafia wine, either because they were made to be eaten with it, or because they were almond flavored. Ratafia was a fruit liqueur, usually based on cherries, peaches, or almonds. It was drunk mid-morning, and considered a great tonic.

Scotch Shortbread

This is a traditional shortbread and very delicious. It is based on Mrs. Beeton's recipe.

A SELECTION OF SHORTBREAD

INGREDIENTS

1 cup Butter
3 cups Flour
1/4 cup Sugar
1/8 cup Caraway Seeds
1/4 cup Chopped Almonds
Candied Peel for Decoration

METHOD

❧ Place the butter in a mixing bowl and cream with a wooden spoon until soft. Add the flour in several stages, beating thoroughly between each addition. Add the sugar, caraway seeds, and almonds and mix to a smooth paste using your hands.

❧ Split the prepared shortbread into three equal pieces and roll each one into a rectangle about 1 inch thick. Prick well with a fork, decorate with a few pieces of candied peel, and place on greased baking sheets.

❧ Cook at 350°F for 25 minutes.

Decorated by Royalty

AT BUCKINGHAM PALACE, THE PATTERN PRICKED ON THE SHORTBREAD WAS ALWAYS THE SAME: THREE ROWS OF THREE DOTS, IN A DOMINO PATTERN.

Balmoral Shortbread

This recipe comes direct from the royal kitchens. Queen Victoria used to eat a little of this delicious shortbread every day.

INGREDIENTS

1 cup Softened Butter
1/2 cup Sugar
2 1/2 cups Flour

METHOD

❧ Place the softened butter and sugar in a bowl and cream together. Sieve in the flour and, using the fingertips, gently work it into the mixture until a dough is formed.

❧ Roll out the bread very thinly and cut into cookies using cutters. Prick the surface of each one with a fork.

❧ Place the finished cookies on a greased baking sheet and cook at 350°F for 15 minutes.

IMPERIALS

These zesty little cakes are based on a recipe from Eliza Acton. She opined that they were "not very rich," and therefore suitable for children. Perhaps they were accompanied by Imperial Water, a kind of lemonade made from water, lemons, and cream of tartar.

INGREDIENTS

3 cups Flour

³/₄ cups Butter

1 cup Sugar

1 cup Currants

¹/₃ cup Chopped Candied Peel

Grated Rind of 1 Lemon

4 Eggs

Learn to think Imperially.
JOSEPH CHAMBERLAIN

METHOD

❧ Using your fingertips, rub the flour and butter together in a bowl. When the mixture resembles fine breadcrumbs, stir in the sugar, currants, chopped peel, and grated lemon rind.

❧ Beat the eggs well in a separate bowl and add them gradually to the mixture until well incorporated. Very lightly grease and flour a baking sheet and, using forks, make small piles of the mixture, remembering to leave enough space between each to allow them to spread during baking.

❧ Cook at 300°F for 20 minutes, until they are an even pale brown color.

DESSERT COOKIES

*These are based on Mrs. Beeton's recipe; they
taste good as they are, but can be flavored in
various ways.*

INGREDIENTS

1/2 cup Butter

1 cup Flour

1/4 cup Ground Ginger

1/2 cup Sugar

2 Egg Yolks, Beaten

MAKES 24 BISCUITS

METHOD

❦ Place the butter in a basin and beat it with a wooden spoon
until soft. Sift the flour and ground ginger together and add it
gradually to the butter, beating in each addition well before adding
the next.

❦ Stir in the sugar and the well-beaten egg yolks and continue to
beat for a few minutes. Cover a baking sheet with a piece of buttered
wax paper and spoon on small amounts of the mixture, leaving
enough space for the biscuits to spread when cooking.

❦ Bake at 300°F for about 20 minutes. Do not let the biscuits
color too much.

Mrs. Beeton suggests THAT YOU
FLAVOR THESE COOKIES BY ADDING LEMON
ESSENCE, GROUND GINGER, CINNAMON, OR
CURRANTS WITH THE SUGAR.
YOU COULD SPLIT THE MIXTURE
IN HALF AND FLAVOR EACH
BATCH DIFFERENTLY.

LIGHT AND TANGY JUMBLES AND LEMON BISCUITS

JUMBLES

These crisp, lemony cookies were an established favorite a century or two before the Victorian era. Earlier recipes referred to them as "jumballs." The recipe given here is based on Eliza Acton's.

Jumbles were made in a ring or in roll shapes. "There were hearts and rounds, and jumbles, which playful youth slip over the forefinger before spoiling their annular outline."

OLIVER WENDELL HOLMES, ELSIE VENNER

INGREDIENTS

3 cups Flour

2 1/4 cup Sugar

4 Eggs

3/4 cup Butter

Grated Rind of 2 Lemons

Freshly Grated Nutmeg

METHOD

❦ Sift the flour and sugar into a bowl. Break the eggs into a separate bowl and beat thoroughly, then add them to the flour and sugar and mix well.

❦ Melt the butter gently over a low heat before adding to the mixture along with the lemon rind and the grated nutmeg. Mix all the ingredients together and drop spoonfuls of the mixture onto greased baking sheets.

❦ Bake at 300°F for 30 minutes until the cookies have become crisp, but are still pale in color.

LEMON COOKIES

These are based on a recipe from Mrs. Beeton. They are very refreshing for afternoon tea, or when served with homemade ice cream or syllabub.

INGREDIENTS

2 1/4 cups Flour

3/4 cup Butter

1 cup Sugar

Grated rind of 1 lemon

4 Eggs

2 t. Fresh Lemon Juice

METHOD

❦ Sift the flour into a mixing bowl and add the butter, cut into small pieces. Using the tips of the fingers, gently rub the fat into the flour before adding the sugar and grated lemon rind.

❦ In a separate bowl, whisk the eggs and lemon juice together, add to the main ingredients, and beat thoroughly. Take spoonfuls of the mixture and drop onto a greased baking sheet, leaving a gap between each to allow for spreading during cooking.

❦ Cook at 350°F for 20 minutes or until the cookies are a delicate shade of brown.

He said that few people had the intellectual resources sufficient to forgo the pleasures of wine. They could not otherwise contrive how to fill the interval between dinner and supper.

JAMES BOSWELL,
THE LIFE OF DR. JOHNSON

WINE CAKES

These delicious wine-flavored cookies are based on a Victorian recipe but have an unmistakeably rakish, 18th-century tang. Try them as sweet snacks to go with wine, or serve them for dessert with Whipped Syllabub and fresh fruit purée.

INGREDIENTS

$^1/_2$ cup Butter
3 to 4 T. Red Wine
1 $^1/_2$ cups Flour
1 cup Sugar
2 Eggs
Caraway Seeds
Beaten Egg to Glaze

METHOD

❦ Soften the butter in a mixing bowl and add the wine a little at a time until well mixed. Mix the flour and sugar and sift into the bowl in stages, stirring between each addition.

❦ Beat the eggs lightly and add to the mixture along with a few caraway seeds to form a firm paste that can be rolled out. Turn the paste out onto a very lightly floured surface and roll out thinly; using the top of a cup or tumbler, cut the cakes from the paste and place on a baking sheet.

❦ Lightly brush the tops with a little beaten egg and sprinkle with sugar. Bake at 425°F for ten minutes, and allow to cool before serving.

The
enthusiastic reception
I met with on the occasion
of my Jubilee has touched
me most deeply.
QUEEN
VICTORIA

THE ROYAL JUBILEES

When *Albert, her beloved husband, died in 1861, Queen Victoria retired from public life. In 1887, the prime minister Benjamin Disraeli persuaded her to publicly celebrate 50 years on the throne with the Golden Jubilee, followed a decade later by the Diamond Jubilee, "a great festival of empire."*

JUBILEE TEA CAKES

Far more sophisticated than their name implies, these can be eaten at teatime, but also make an impressive dessert when served with a little ice cream. This is based on an authentic Victorian recipe, perhaps invented to celebrate the two Royal Jubilees of 1887 and 1897.

INGREDIENTS

5 T. Fresh Cream
3 to 4 T. Water
¼ cup Butter
⅛ cup Sugar
1 cup Ground Almonds
4 Eggs
Vanilla Essence
1½ cups Confectioner's Sugar
1 to 2 T. Water
Almond Flavoring
Fresh Fruit to Garnish

Hurrah! Hurrah! We bring the Jubilee!
H.G. WORK,
MARCHING THROUGH GEORGIA

METHOD

❧ Place the cream, 3 to 4 T. water, butter, and sugar in a saucepan and bring to the boil. Once boiling, add the ground almonds and stir well to incorporate them into the liquid; reduce the heat to a simmer and allow the mixture to cook for a few minutes.

❧ Separate the eggs and beat the yolks with a few drops of vanilla essence, then take the almond mixture from the heat and slowly add it to the egg yolks, beating well all the time. Take two of the egg whites, whisk them until they form stiff peaks, and carefully fold them into the prepared mixture.

❧ Grease a ring mold and line it with wax paper, dust lightly with a little flour and pour in the cake mixture. Bake at 350°F for about 25 minutes, until the cake has turned a pale brown color. Remove the cake from the mold and place on a wire rack to cool.

❧ To make the icing, sift the confectioner's sugar into a bowl and add the water a little at a time until the icing is smooth and of the correct consistency. Add a few drops of almond flavoring and pour over the cake only when it has completely cooled. Garnish with fresh fruit such as sliced apple.

THREADNEEDLE STREET COOKIES

This is recipe is based on one from Eliza Acton. It produces austere, dignified, semi-sweet cookies, rather like digestives, that would have been very suitable for the sober junketings of bankers and shareholders.

INGREDIENTS

6 ½ cups Flour
⅓ cup Butter
½ cup Sugar
Caraway Seeds (Optional)
Milk

METHOD

❧ Sift the flour into a large mixing bowl, add the butter and rub through using the fingertips until it resembles fine breadcrumbs. Sift the sugar into the basin and add a few caraway seeds if desired; stir together well.

❧ Adding a little milk at a time, stir the mixture with a wooden spoon until it forms a firm paste that is suitable for rolling out. Turn the paste out onto a lightly floured work surface and knead until it is very smooth, then roll it out until it is about ⅓ inch thick. Cut the cookies out using small, square cutters, and place them on baking sheets.

❧ Bake at 300°F until the cookies are crisp all over. When cooked, remove them from the oven and cool on wire racks prior to serving.

THE BANK OF ENGLAND *is known as the Old Lady of Threadneedle Street, which is where it stands in the City of London.*

THREADNEEDLE STREET BISCUITS

Harris and I would go down in the morning. . .and George, who would not be able to get away from the City till the afternoon (George goes to sleep at a bank from ten to four each day, except Saturdays, when they wake him up and put him outside at two), would meet us there.

J. K. JEROME,
THREE MEN IN A BOAT

Caraway Seeds

Victorian cooks used caraway seeds liberally in cakes, candies, and cookies. Perhaps the attraction was medicinal; caraway seeds are reputed to aid the digestion and combat flatulence.

MEREWORTH BISCUITS

These are light, crisp crackers to eat buttered or with soft cheese. The recipe is based on one from Lady Sarah Lindsay's Choice Recipes (1883). Mereworth, where they were first made, is a stately home in Kent.

INGREDIENTS

1²/₃ cups Plain Flour
Pinch of Salt
¹/₈ cup Butter
Hot Milk

COOK'S TIP

This recipe produces a great number of biscuits so storing them in an air-tight tin until required is a good idea.

METHOD

❧ Add a pinch of salt to the flour and sift it into a bowl. Rub the butter into the flour and slowly add enough hot milk to make a soft dough.

❧ Turn the dough out onto a lightly floured surface and knead well for a few minutes. Take small amounts of the dough, roll out very thinly, and cut into rounds using a plain cutter.

❧ Place on baking sheets and cook at 425°F until they have browned and risen a little.

The Stately homes of England
How beautiful they stand
Amidst their tall ancestral trees
O'er all the pleasant land!

FELICIA HEMANS

FINE WHITE BREAD BISCUITS

These are based on a recipe from Eliza Acton called Aunt Charlotte's Biscuits; she describes them as "very simple and very good." Use them as you would use salted crackers.

COOK'S TIP

If you are making white bread, use up surplus dough by making these biscuits, kneading 1oz butter into each 1lb of dough after it has risen.

INGREDIENTS

$^1/_4$ *cup Fresh Yeast*

$3^3/_4$ *cups Warm Water*

$9^1/_2$ *cups Flour*

2 t. Salt

$^1/_8$ *cup Sugar*

$^2/_3$ *cup Butter*

METHOD

❧ Put the yeast in a bowl and stir in a little of the warm water. Put to one side for ten minutes to froth. Sift the flour and salt together into a mixing bowl, add the sugar, and rub in a little less than half of the butter. Using your hand, stir in the frothing yeast mixture and the rest of the warm water to produce a soft dough. Knead for a few minutes on a floured board, cover, and place in a warm cupboard for $1^1/_2$ hours until it has doubled in size.

❧ Once the dough has proven, turn it out onto the board and knock the air out by kneading it again. Break the remaining butter into small pieces and work them thoroughly into the dough.

❧ Leave for another 30 minutes to rise again, then flatten the dough out until it is roughly $^1/_4$ inch thick. Prick all over with a fork and cut out the biscuits using cutters. Place on baking sheets and cook at 350°F for about ten minutes.

GINGERBREAD

This is based on Andrew's Gingerbread, one of Mrs Beeton's many gingerbread recipes. This is a quick, simple recipe, ideal for children to cook themselves.

INGREDIENTS

4 cups Plain Flour
1/2 cup Sugar
3/4 cup Butter
2 Eggs
1/4 cup Ground Ginger
3/4 cup Corn Syrup

METHOD

❦ Place the butter, sugar, and syrup into a bowl and beat until well creamed together. Beat the eggs one at a time and add to the mixture, ensuring they are well mixed in.

❦ Sift together the ginger and flour and slowly add to the bowl, stirring all the time, until the bread is very thick.

❦ Roll out the gingerbread thinly on a lightly floured board and cut into cookies using cutters. Bake at 350°F for about 20 to 25 minutes, until the biscuits have hardened and are darker in color.

THE GILT ON THE GINGERBREAD

Gingerbread has a long history. In medieval times, it was made with honey, cooked in dark brown slabs and studded with gilded leaves and cloves to look like the tooled leather worn by noble knights.

Our boyish days look very merry to us now, all nutting, hoop, and gingerbread.

J.K. JEROME
IDLE THOUGHTS OF AN
IDLE FELLOW

RICH GINGERBREAD NUTS

These are very dressy ginger nuts, based on Mrs. Beeton's recipe. They are delicious for a special occasion tea, or as a gift for gingerbread fans.

INGREDIENTS

1/2 cup Butter
1 1/3 cups Molasses
2 1/4 cups Coarse Brown Sugar
1/4 cup Ground Ginger
1/2 cup Chopped Candied Peel
3 T. Ground Caraway Seeds
1 Egg
Flour

METHOD

❦ Place the butter in a small pan and warm over a low heat until it has just melted. Pass the melted butter through a clean piece of muslin to remove any impurities. Pour the clarified butter into a basin containing the molasses and add to it the brown sugar and the ground ginger.

❦ Mix together well, stirring in the chopped peel and ground caraway seeds as you mix. Add the egg and enough flour, a little at a time, until a good, stiff paste is formed.

❦ Strew some flour over a board and roll out the gingerbread evenly, then cut into any shapes you desire and place on greased baking sheets. Bake at 325°F for 30 minutes.

THICK GINGERBREAD

This recipe, based on Mrs. Beeton's, produces rich, thick slabs of spicy gingerbread. Children love it; it's very good for bonfire parties or Halloween.

INGREDIENTS

1 1/3 cups Molasses
1/2 cup Butter
1/2 cup Soft Brown Sugar
4 3/4 cups Flour
1/4 cup Ground Ginger
1/8 cup Ground Allspice
1/8 cup Bicarbonate of Soda
2/3 cup Warm Milk
3 Eggs
1 Egg Yolk for Glazing

METHOD

❦ Sift the flour into a large basin and mix in the brown sugar, ginger, and allspice. Melt the butter and molasses over a low heat and stir into the other ingredients along with the bicarbonate of soda dissolved in the warm milk.

❦ Lightly whisk the eggs and beat into the gingerbread until a smooth dough is formed.

❦ Pour the mixture into a greased pan and cook at 350°F for approximately one hour. A few minutes before the cooking is complete, brush the top with beaten egg and return it to the oven.

THICK GINGERBREAD TO SWEETEN
LAZY SUNDAY AFTERNOONS.

SAVOY CAKE

This is based on Mrs. Beeton's recipe. According to her, it is "a very nice cake for dessert, and may be iced for a supper table, or cut into slices and spread with jam."

INGREDIENTS

6 Eggs
1 cup Sugar
Grated Rind Of 1 Lemon
Almond Essence
2 1/3 cups Flour

METHOD

❧ Separate the eggs and beat the yolks with the sugar, lemon rind, and a few drops of almond essence.

❧ In a clean bowl, whisk the egg whites until they form peaks and fold them into the yolks. Beat together well with a whisk for a few minutes, then sift in the flour and fold into the mixture.

❧ Pour the mixture into a greased and floured loose-bottomed pan and bake at 350°F for 1 1/2 hours or until a skewer inserted into the cake comes out cleanly.

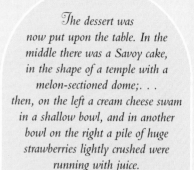

The dessert was now put upon the table. In the middle there was a Savoy cake, in the shape of a temple with a melon-sectioned dome;. . . then, on the left a cream cheese swam in a shallow bowl, and in another bowl on the right a pile of huge strawberries lightly crushed were running with juice.

EMILE ZOLA, L'ASSOMMOIR

SAVOY COOKIES

Savoy Cookies are delectable on their own, but also form an intrinsic part of complicated dishes such as Charlotte Russe and Cabinet Pudding. This recipe is based on Mrs. Beeton's.

INGREDIENTS

4 Eggs
1 cup Sugar
Rind of 1 Lemon
1 cup Flour

METHOD

❧ Separate the eggs, place the yolks in a mixing bowl, and beat well. Add the sugar and lemon rind and continue beating for a good ten minutes. Slowly add the flour to the bowl a little at a time and beat thoroughly between each addition.

❧ In a clean bowl, whisk the egg whites until they form stiff peaks and fold them into the biscuit mixture before beating all the ingredients together briefly.

❧ Take spoonfuls of the mixture and allow it to run onto greased baking sheets to form finger shapes. Bake at 350°F until lightly browned, but do keep a watchful eye, as they cook quickly and can burn soon after.

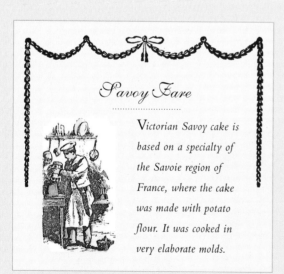

Savoy Fare

Victorian Savoy cake is based on a specialty of the Savoie region of France, where the cake was made with potato flour. It was cooked in very elaborate molds.

LIGHT AND GOLDEN SAVOY CAKES AND SAVOY BISCUITS

MADEIRA CAKE

This cake was made to be eaten with Madeira wine when visitors called in the late morning. It is just as enjoyable at the tea table. This recipe is based on Eliza Acton's "A Good Madeira Cake."

COOK'S TIP

A light dusting of confectioner's sugar prior to serving finishes this delicious, tangy cake

INGREDIENTS

1 cup Sugar
¹/₂ cup Butter
4 Eggs
Grated Rind of 1 Lemon
1 cup Flour
Pinch of Salt

METHOD

❦ Put the butter and sugar in a bowl and cream together until light in color. Beat in the eggs one at a time and add the grated lemon rind.

❦ Sift the flour and salt into the basin and gently fold into the cake mixture using a wooden spoon.

❦ Pour the prepared cake mixture into a well-greased, loose-bottomed cake pan and bake at 350°F for 1¹/₂ hours, until nicely browned on top.

MADEIRA WINE

<u>MADEIRA</u> is one of the finest of the fortified dessert wines. It comes from Madeira, made from grapes grown on vines imported to the island from Cyprus in the 15th century. It is very sweet to today's taste, but was a great favorite with the Victorians.

MADEIRA CAKE TO PARTNER MADEIRA WINE

SPONGECAKE

*This is an old-fashioned spongecake, feathery and light
because it contains no fat. The cake is suitable for cooking in
fanciful molds or as a basis for such sweet delights as Hedgehog
Pudding. This is based on Mrs. Beeton's recipe.*

INGREDIENTS

1 cup Sugar
4 Eggs
Grated Rind Of 1 Lemon
1 cup Flour

COOK'S TIP

The air incorporated into the egg
whites is a major factor in this
cake's lightness, so do be gentle
during the preparation.

METHOD

❧ Separate the eggs and lightly beat the yolks. Place them in a
saucepan with the sugar and place over a gentle heat. Stir until the
sugar has dissolved but do not allow the pan to get too hot.

❧ Take the mixture from the heat and pour it into a bowl, add the
grated lemon rind, and mix well. Sift in the flour in several stages,
stirring well between each addition, and fold in the egg whites, which
have been whisked to stiff-peak stage.

❧ Beat the cake mixture well for a few minutes, then pour it into a
loose-bottomed cake pan that has been greased and sprinkled with
sugar. Bake the cake immediately at 350°F for 1$\frac{1}{2}$ hours.

TRADITIONAL SPONGE CAKE
AND VICTORIA SANDWICH

VICTORIA SANDWICH

*This variation on the spongecake, named
for the Queen, is based on Mrs. Beeton's recipe.*

INGREDIENTS

1 cup Butter	*Grated Rind of 1 Lemon*
1 cup Sugar	*Your Favorite Jam*
4 Eggs	*for Filling*
1 $\frac{2}{3}$ cups Flour	*Confectioner's Sugar*
Pinch Of Salt	

METHOD

❧ Place the butter and sugar in a bowl and beat with a wooden spoon
until pale and soft. Beat in the eggs one at a time until well incorporated.

❧ Fold in the sifted flour and salt and add the grated lemon rind. Stir
for a few minutes then pour the cake mixture into a greased cake pan
and bake for 20 minutes at 350°F.

❧ When the cake is firm to the touch, remove it from the oven and
cool on a wire rack. Split the cake through the middl,fill with jam and
cut into fingers. Serve immediately, dusted with confectioner's sugar.

It was the Victorian cooks WHO INTRODUCED THE
IDEA OF ADDING BUTTER TO THE TRADITIONAL
ENGLISH SPONGECAKE MIXTURE; THIS PRODUCED A
MORE SOLID MIX THAT BAKED RATHER FLATTER.
THE RESULTING CAKES COULD BE SANDWICHED
TOGETHER TO CONSTRUCT THE KIND OF "BUILT
CAKE," SO SATISFYING THE ENGINEERING
MENTALITY OF MANY VICTORIANS.

ITALIAN MERINGUES

These are based on Eliza Acton's recipe. They are intended to be fastened together with whipped cream.

COOK'S TIP

Use a kitchen fork to flick melted chocolate over the finished meringues to produce very attractive results.

INGREDIENTS

2 1/4 cups Sugar
2 1/2 cups Fresh Water
4 Egg Whites

METHOD

❧ Place the sugar and water in a saucepan and boil until the solution starts to turn white in the pan. Turn off the heat and allow it to stand for 2 to 3 minutes, stirring continuously to keep the sugar soft.

❧ Beat the egg whites until they form stiff peaks, then quickly combine the sugar and egg whites to form a meringue that can hold its shape when molded.

❧ Take teaspoonfuls of meringue and place on baking sheets. Cook the meringues in a very slow oven, 250°F, until they have hardened but show no signs of coloring.

THE ROYAL CONNECTION

Meringues are said to have been invented in 1720 by a Swiss pastry cook named Gasparini. At the time, he was working in Mehrinyghen, a town in Saxe-Coburg-Gotha, the birthplace of both Queen Victoria's beloved consort Albert, and her mother, Victoria Louise.

Let them eat Meringue

MARIE-ANTOINETTE, THE DOOMED QUEEN OF FRANCE, MADE HER OWN MERINGUES IN HER PLAY-KITCHEN AT LE PETIT TRIANON PALACE AT VERSAILLES.

Sweet King

THE FIRST MERINGUES made in France were offered to Duke Stanislaus of Lorraine, the deposed King of Poland and father in law of Louis XV. Stanislaus was a connoisseur of sweet things; he is credited with the invention of the Rum Baba.

MERINGUES

These are rather lighter Italian meringues, based on sugar syrup; these are based on Mrs. Beeton's recipe. You can pile them altogether to make a glorious dessert.

INGREDIENTS

4 Egg Whites
1 cup Sugar
Fresh Heavy Cream
Fresh Soft Fruit to Garnish (Optional)

He insisted on her partaking of a large glass of lemonade and three meringues.

MRS CATTYN,
THE QUAKER GRANDMOTHER

COOK'S TIP

When whisking, it is most important that the mixture is treated carefully, as the more air incorporated into the mixture, the lighter the meringues will be.

METHOD

❧ Place the egg whites in a clean bowl and whisk until they form stiff peaks. Using a metal spoon, take one tablespoonful of the sugar and stir lightly into the egg whites. Continue whisking the meringue and slowly add the remaining sugar.

❧ Cover a baking tray with wax paper and lightly oil the surface. Take tablespoonfuls of the meringue and place them a small distance apart and roughly the same size on the paper. Bake in a very cool oven, 250°F, for 2 hours until they begin to color.

❧ Remove them from the oven and allow to cool before sandwiching them together with some fresh whipped cream and decorating with fresh raspberries or slices of fresh strawberry.

LIGHT AND LUSCIOUS MERINGUES

SEED CAKE

Seed Cake or Seedy Cake is a traditional country cake, often eaten at harvest time, but popular all the year round. This is based on Mrs. Beeton's recipe for a "Very Good Seed Cake," and makes a deliciously moist cake.

INGREDIENTS

2 cups Butter
3 cups Flour
1³/₄ cups Sugar
1 T. Caraway Seeds
3 to 4 T. Brandy
6 Eggs
Grated Nutmeg

COOK'S TIP

This cake would be equally good made with currants instead of caraway seeds, according to Mrs. Beeton.

METHOD

❦ Place the butter in a mixing bowl and beat until soft with a wooden spoon. Sift in the flour and add the sugar, caraway seeds, and a little grated nutmeg, and mix thoroughly.

❦ Break the eggs into a separate bowl, beat lightly, and add to the cake mixture along with the brandy. Beat all the ingredients together for a few minutes, then pour into a lightly greased, loose-based cake pan.

❦ Cook at 350°F for 1¹/₂ hours.

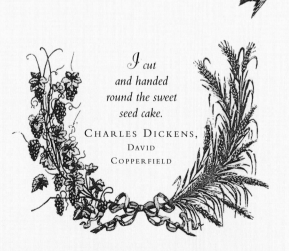

I cut and handed round the sweet seed cake.

CHARLES DICKENS,
DAVID
COPPERFIELD

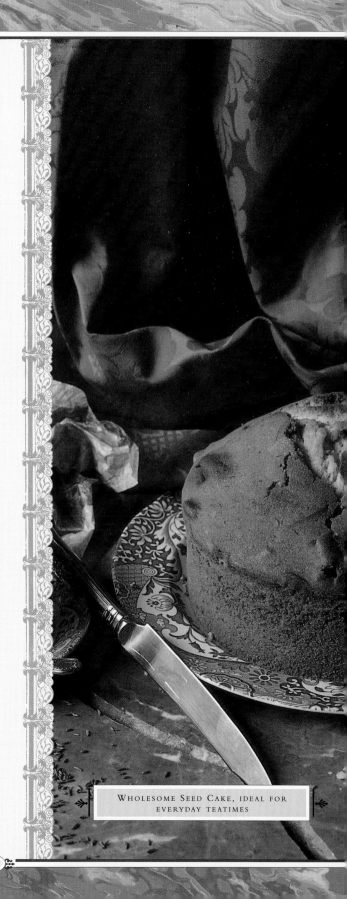

WHOLESOME SEED CAKE, IDEAL FOR EVERYDAY TEATIMES

SPICY SYRUP AND RAISIN CAKE

This is based on a recipe of Mrs. Beeton's called "Aunt Betsey's Cake." You can just imagine an indulgent auntie making this delicious, sticky fruitcake for her favorite nieces and nephews.

INGREDIENTS

¼ cup Butter

1 cup Sugar

2 Eggs

1t. Bicarbonate of Soda

⅕pt Cold Water

3 cups Flour

5 T. Corn Syrup

1½ cups Raisins

Pinch of Cinnamon, Ground Cloves
and Ground Mace

COOK'S TIP

You can use this mixture to make small cakes in muffin pans if a large one is impractical.

METHOD

❦ Place the butter and sugar in a mixing bowl and cream together until light in color. Add the eggs one at a time and beat into the mixture until well incorporated.

❦ Dissolve the bicarbonate of soda in the cold water and add along with the remaining ingredients; beat together thoroughly for a few minutes.

❦ Turn the cake mixture into a well-greased square cake pan and bake at 350°F for 1½ hours.

CORN SYRUP WAS FIRST MADE IN THE 1880s. IT WAS PRODUCED AS A BY-PRODUCT DURING THE REFINING PROCESS OF CRYSTALLIZED SUGAR.

COCONUT CAKE

An elaborate coconut extravaganza, this cake is based on a recipe from Mrs. Beeton.

INGREDIENTS

³/₄ cup Butter

1 cup Sugar

2 Eggs

3 cups Flour

2¹/₂ t. Baking Powder

4oz Shredded Coconut

Grated Lemon Rind

A little Milk

Chocolate Icing for Decoration (see page 33)

Jam

Shredded Coconut for Decoration

METHOD

❧ Place the butter and sugar together in a bowl and cream until pale in color. Beat in the eggs one at a time and sift in the flour and baking powder. Add the shredded coconut and grated lemon rind and mix together well.

❧ Slowly add enough milk to bring the cake mixture to a batter-like consistency and divide it equally between two buttered cake pans. Bake at 350°F for about 25 minutes until well risen and golden, then cool on wire racks.

❧ Sandwich the two halves together with a thick layer of jam, and make a chocolate icing to coat the top of the cake. Melt a little more jam, brush over the sides of the cake, and sprinkle with handfuls of coconut to decorate.

COCONUT ROCKS

As you may gather from their name, these are rather more robust than Coconut Cookies. The recipe is based on one from Mrs. Beeton.

INGREDIENTS

¹/₂ cup Butter

¹/₂ cup Sugar

³/₄ cup Flour

3oz Shredded Coconut

2 Eggs

METHOD

❧ Cream the butter and sugar together until light and fluffy. Slowly sift in the flour and add the coconut, beating between each addition.

❧ Break the eggs into a bowl and whisk lightly before beating into the cake mixture.

❧ Using a spoon, drop small amounts of the mixture onto greased baking sheets and bake at 425°F for ten minutes.

COCONUTS

Coconuts were imported from the Caribbean and were extremely popular in the 19th century. Victorian cooks used them for cakes, cookies, candies, and puddings; shredded coconut was a very popular garnish.

DELICIOUS AND AROMATIC COFFEE CAKES

COFFEE CAKES`

*D*elicious with morning coffee or hot chocolate, these
delicate little cakes are based on a genuine, but unattributed, Victorian recipe.

INGREDIENTS

4 Eggs

1 cup Sugar

2½ t. Strong Coffee Granules

1 t. Baking Powder

¾ cup Flour

*C*offee, which makes the politician wise
And see through all things with
his half-shut eyes.

ALEXANDER POPE,
THE RAPE OF THE LOCK

Coffee in an Instant

*The original Victorian recipe used
made-up coffee. Instant coffee was invented
by G. W. Washington, an Englishman living
in Guatemala, who noticed that when
steaming coffee cooled on the coffee pot
spout, it produced a fine powder. He
worked on a method to reproduce this
commercially, and in 1909,
instant coffee was created.*

METHOD

❧ Break the four eggs into a bowl and add the coffee and sugar. Place the bowl over a saucepan of boiling water and whisk the contents until they have warmed. Remove the bowl and continue whisking until the mixture has cooled and become thick.

❧ Mix the baking powder into the flour and allow to warm a little in a very low oven. Gradually add it to the coffee mixture in several stages, mixing well between each addition. Pour the prepared cake mixture into cake pans that have been lightly buttered and floured, and bake at 350°F for about 15 minutes.

❧ Remove them from the oven and turn out onto racks to cool. Dust with a little confectioner's sugar or coat with a coffee icing and serve.

Fine Almond Cake

This cake is based on a recipe from Eliza Acton. It is gorgeously rich but very refined, so a little goes a very long way.

INGREDIENTS

2 cups Fresh Almonds

12 Eggs

2¼ cups Sugar

2½ cups Flour

2 cups Butter

Grated Rind of 2 Lemons

METHOD

❧ Blanch the almonds to remove their skins, then grind them to a paste in a mortar and pestle and put them in a large mixing bowl. Break the dozen eggs into a separate bowl and whisk until very light and fluffy, then gradually mix them into the ground almonds.

❧ Mix together the sugar and flour and add to the basin in several stages, stopping to beat the mixture between each addition. Gently melt the butter in a saucepan and pour it through a piece of clean muslin to remove any sediment. Add the purified butter to the cake mixture in stages, beating very thoroughly to incorporate it before adding any more.

❧ When all the butter has been added, mix in the grated lemon rind and pour the mixture into a well-buttered cake tin. Bake at 400°F for two hours.

Almond Overload

True fans of almonds might like to follow Eliza Acton's suggestion and add an extra $^3/_4$ cup of blanched almonds to the mixture, in which case additional sugar ($^1/_4$ cup) and an extra egg will be needed.

COOK'S TIP

If the cake colors quickly, cover it with a piece of wax paper to prevent it browning any more.

FINE ALMOND CAKE, VERY RICH AND VERY REFINED

PLAIN POUNDCAKE

Poundcake traditionally means any kind of cake made with equal proportions of flour, sugar, and butter or fat. This version is based on Eliza Acton's recipe. You can add various ingredients to make your own family version.

INGREDIENTS

1 1/2 cups Flour

1 cup Sugar

1 cup Butter

5 Eggs

METHOD

❧ Beat the butter to a cream in a mixing bowl, add the sugar, and continue beating until well mixed in. Separate the eggs and beat the yolks into the butter in several stages.

❧ In a separate bowl beat the egg whites until they are stiff, then spoon them into the mixing bowl and gently mix them into the cake. Sift the flour into the mixing bowl a little at a time, and stir into the cake mixture.

❧ Pour the mixture into a buttered cake pan and cook at 350°F for an hour, until well risen and nicely browned.

POUND CAKE, THE CENTREPIECE OF THE FARMHOUSE TEA-TABLE

Queen Cakes

THESE ARE SMALL CAKES, USUALLY HEART-SHAPED, MADE FROM THE MIXTURE INDICATED FOR POUND CURRANT CAKE. SERVED WITH CIDER, THEY WERE A SPECIALTY OF VARIOUS LONDON INNS IN THE 18TH CENTURY.

COOK'S TIP

Eliza Acton turns this into Pound Currant Cake by adding 1 1/4 cups currants and some candied peel before the flour is added. The recipe can also be turned into Irish Speckled Bread with the simple addition of caraway seeds.

He begged to recommend the pound cake from his own personal experience.

FRANCES TROLLOPE,
CHARMING FELLOWS

It will have a great odour of bohea and pound cake.

WILLIAM THACKERAY,
MEN & COATS

CHOCOLATE SURPRISE

This lovely, light cake is based on a recipe from Lady Shaftesbury, who calls it Surprise au Chocolat. The surprise happens when you cut the dark, chocolatey outside to reveal a pale, creamy inside.

INGREDIENTS

6 Eggs

1 cup Sugar

⅓ cup Flour

½ cup Cornstarch

1¼ cup Cream, Whipped

4 squares Unsweetened Chocolate

⅛ cup Unsalted Butter

1 cup Confectioner's Sugar

3–4 T. Water

Chocolate for Grating

METHOD

❧ Separate the eggs and beat the yolks to a smooth paste with the sugar. Sift the flour and cornstarch into the bowl and fold into the mixture.

❧ In a sterilized bowl, whisk the egg whites until they form stiff peaks and fold them into the cake mixture. Line a 9-inch loose-bottomed cake pan with wax paper and gently pour in the cake mixture. Bake at 350°F for 45 minutes.

❧ Allow the cake to cool for a few minutes, then carefully remove it from the tin and stand it on a wire rack to cool completely. Once cold, cut the cake in half, remove some of the crumbs from inside the two halves, and fill the holes with the stiffly whipped cream.

❧ Sandwich the cake back together again and cover completely with the icing. Decorate the finished cake with a little grated chocolate and chill before serving.

COOK'S TIP

It is essential that egg whites are folded into the mixture with the utmost care, as the more air incorporated into the cake, the lighter it will be.

CHOCOLATE ICING

Break up the chocolate and place it in a bowl over a saucepan of simmering water to melt. Add the butter, cut into small pieces, stir in the confectioner's sugar, and continue stirring until smooth. Remove from the heat and add the water, allow the icing a little time to cool.

Eating Chocolate

Surprise au Chocolat would have been a very modern, sophisticated cake. Sweet chocolate for eating was not made until 1847, when it was invented by Fry & Sons in England. Milk chocolate was developed in Switzerland in 1876. In the 17th and 18th centuries, chocolate was bitter, and only used for drinking.

CHOCOLATE SURPRISE
TO DELIGHT DINNER GUESTS

SODA CAKE

◦⧴⧵◦

A wholesome cake based on a recipe from Eliza Acton, who disapproved of rich cakes. It is economical and easy to make, ideal for daily consumption.

COOK'S TIP

You can split the mixture in half to make two smaller cakes; in this case, the cooking time should be 45 minutes.

INGREDIENTS

3 cups Flour
³⁄₄ cup Butter
1 cup Sugar
²⁄₃ cup Milk
3 Eggs, Beaten
Grated Rind of 1 Lemon
1¹⁄₄ cups Currants
Good Pinch of Bicarbonate of Soda

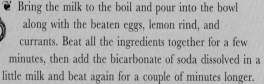

METHOD

❦ Sift the flour into a mixing bowl and rub through the butter, using the tips of the fingers, until the mixture resembles fine breadcrumbs. Sift in the sugar and stir until well incorporated.

❦ Bring the milk to the boil and pour into the bowl along with the beaten eggs, lemon rind, and currants. Beat all the ingredients together for a few minutes, then add the bicarbonate of soda dissolved in a little milk and beat again for a couple of minutes longer.

❦ Pour the mixture into a well-greased mold and cook at 350°F for 1¹⁄₄ hours. Insert a skewer into the center of the cake; if it comes out cleanly, then the cake is ready.

If carefully made, it resembles a poundcake, but is much less expensive and far more wholesome, while it has the advantage of being very expeditiously prepared.

ELIZA ACTON
ON SODA CAKE

BAKING SODA

Eliza Acton warns against "too large a proportion, or a course quality of soda," as either will make the cake disagreeable. Bicarbonate of Soda, which produces carbon dioxide when mixed with liquid, was introduced as a raising agent in cooking in the mid-19th century.

Lawn Tennis

LAWN TENNIS is a 19th-century adaptation of the ancient royal game of tennis. It was developed in 1873 by Major Walter Wingfield, who called it "Sphairistike." The All England Croquet Club of Wimbledon took it up with enthusiasm, even adding the name Lawn Tennis to their title; the Club sponsored the first World Lawn Tennis Championship in 1877.

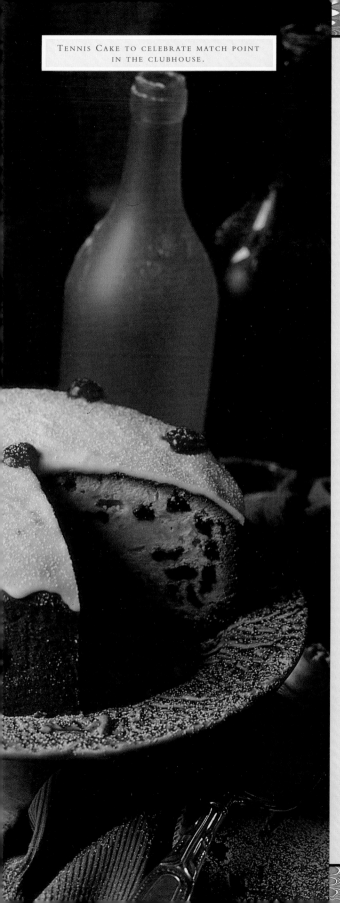

TENNIS CAKE TO CELEBRATE MATCH POINT
IN THE CLUBHOUSE.

TENNIS CAKE

Lawn tennis mania swept late Victorian England, and tennis clubs sprang up all over suburbia. Substantial teas were required in the pavilion after strenuous sets; cucumber sandwiches and a rich cake like this one, adapted from Mrs. Beeton's recipe.

INGREDIENTS

1 cup Sugar

1½ cups Butter

Grated Rind and Juice of 1 Lemon

5 Eggs

3 cups Flour

1½ cups Raisins

1½ cups Chopped Blanched Almonds

½ cup Chopped Candied Peel

⅔ cup Milk

Icing for Decoration

Glacé Cherries

METHOD

❦ Put the sugar and butter into a clean basin and cream together until the mixture is light in color. Beat in the lemon juice and grated rind, and add the eggs individually, beating each one into the mixture thoroughly before adding the next.

❦ When all the eggs have been incorporated, sift in the flour and add the raisins, almonds, and candied peel, and mix well. If the mixture is a little stiff, use some of the milk to bring it to a more batter-like consistency.

❦ Line a loose-bottomed cake pan with wax paper and brush with melted butter. Pour in the cake mixture and bake at 350°F for 1½ hours. Turn the finished cake out onto a wire rack to cool before decorating with white icing and glacé cherries.

> And now came the brief bright season of rustic entertainments...lawn tennis – archery – water parties.
>
> MARY ELIZABETH BRADDON,
> MT ROYAL

PLUM CAKE

Plum Cake was a staple at the Victorian tea table; there are as many recipes as there are cooks, but this one is based on Mrs. Beeton's "Nice Plum Cake."

INGREDIENTS

3 cups Flour

1 cup Sugar

1 1/2 cups Currants

1/3 cup Chopped Candied Peel

1/2 cup Butter

1 1/4 cups Milk

1 t. Bicarbonate of Soda

1 to 2 T. Milk

METHOD

❦ Sift the flour into a mixing bowl and add the sugar, currants, and candied peel. In a separate bowl beat the butter until soft. Add to the other ingredients and bind the whole together with the 1 1/4 cups of milk.

❦ Make a paste using the bicarbonate of soda and remaining milk; add to the cake mixture and beat thoroughly for a few minutes until all of the ingredients are well combined.

❦ Turn the dough into a well-buttered pan and bake at 350°F for 1 1/2 hours.

THE LION AND THE UNICORN

The Lion and the Unicorn were fighting for the crown;
The Lion beat the Unicorn all round the town.
Some gave them white bread, some gave them brown;
Some gave them plum-cake and drummed them out of town.

NURSERY RHYME

PLUM CAKE, THE TRADITIONAL FAVORITE

CHRISTMAS CAKE, THE CENTERPIECE
OF THE FESTIVE TEA TABLE

CHRISTMAS CAKE

The *Victorian family Christmas was not complete without a glorious, rich, and enormous Christmas cake. This is based on Mrs. Beeton's "Christmas Cake No. 1." She advises that it can be baked "in one or more cakes as desired," as it makes such a huge quantity. You can make the cakes six weeks before Christmas, as long as you keep them wrapped in foil and stored in tins.*

COOK'S TIP

Cover the cake with a sheet of wax paper during the second half of its cooking time to prevent the top from burning.

INGREDIENTS

1 cup Butter
1 cup Sugar
4 Eggs
3 cups Flour
4 T. Baking Powder
1 1/3 cups Sultanas
1 1/3 cups Currants
1 cup Chopped Mixed Peel
Milk

METHOD

❧ In a large mixing bowl, cream together the butter and sugar until pale in color. Add the eggs individually, making sure each is thoroughly beaten into the butter before adding the next.

❧ Mix together the flour and baking powder and pass them through a sieve twice to ensure the baking powder is evenly distributed throughout the flour. Add to the cake and mix well, then add the fruit and chopped peel and beat thoroughly. Carefully pour enough milk to the mixture to moisten it to a good batter-like consistency.

❧ Line a good-sized cake pan with wax paper and grease it thoroughly. You may prefer to use two or more cake pans, as this recipe makes almost 4lb. of cake. Pour in the cake, smooth over the surface, and bake at 300°F for 3 to 4 hours.

INDEX